The Gig Econo
Handł

Turning Side Gigs into Gold Mines

Dominic Bates

The Gig Economy Investor's Handbook
© Copyright 2023 by Dominic Bates
All rights reserved

TABLE OF CONTENTS

CHAPTER 1: INTRODUCTION TO THE GIG ECONOMY

The landscape of work is undergoing a seismic shift, and at the heart of this transformation is the rise of the gig economy. In this chapter, we embark on a journey to understand the dynamics, embrace the flexibility, and trace the evolution of gig work from mere freelancing to a realm of investment possibilities.

Understanding the Rise of the Gig Economy

The gig economy, often referred to as the freelance or on-demand economy, has emerged as a powerhouse in the contemporary job market.

Understanding its rise requires delving into the changing nature of work, driven by technological advancements, a quest for flexibility, and a desire for autonomy.

Technology, particularly digital platforms and connectivity, has been a driving force behind the gig economy's ascent. The ease of connecting gig workers with consumers through apps and online platforms has revolutionized how services are delivered. From ride-sharing services to freelance writing gigs, the digital landscape has created a marketplace where skills meet demand with unprecedented efficiency.

Flexibility is a cornerstone of the gig economy, offering individuals the autonomy to shape their work around their lives, rather than the other way around. Embracing gigs means escaping the traditional 9-to-5 constraints, allowing workers to choose when, where, and how they work. This newfound freedom has given rise to a diverse workforce, ranging from full-time freelancers to part-time gig workers supplementing their income.

The gig economy is not just a response to the demands of workers; it's a reflection of changing consumer behaviors. Consumers now seek instant access to services, and the gig economy provides precisely that. Whether it's getting a ride, hiring a graphic designer, or finding someone to assemble furniture, the gig economy has become synonymous with convenience and immediacy.

Embracing the Flexibility of Side Gigs

One of the most alluring aspects of the gig economy is the flexibility it offers to individuals looking to augment their income with side gigs. Embracing this flexibility is about recognizing the potential for financial empowerment and personal fulfillment outside the confines of traditional employment.

Side gigs, often pursued alongside a primary job or other commitments, provide a unique avenue for individuals to explore their passions, develop skills, and generate additional income. The gig economy allows for a diversified approach to work, enabling individuals to engage in multiple projects simultaneously, harnessing a variety of skills and talents.

Flexibility in side gigs extends beyond the work schedule—it encompasses the ability to choose the type of work that aligns with personal interests and expertise. Whether it's graphic design, content creation, or providing specialized services, gig workers have the autonomy to curate a portfolio of work that resonates with their skills and passions.

Moreover, side gigs serve as a safety net in an era of economic uncertainty. Having multiple income streams offers a degree of financial security, reducing dependence on a single source of income. This flexibility is particularly valuable in times of job market volatility or unexpected life events.

The Evolution of Gig Work: From Freelancing to Investing

As the gig economy matures, it undergoes a profound evolution from simple freelancing to a realm of investment opportunities. What began as a means for individuals to offer their skills on a short-term basis has evolved into a dynamic ecosystem where gig workers can transform their efforts into investments with lasting financial impact.

Freelancing, the foundational element of the gig economy, involves providing services on a project or contractual basis. Freelancers, whether in creative fields, IT, or consulting, operate as independent entities, navigating a landscape that rewards skill, reputation, and adaptability. This evolution from traditional employment structures allows gig workers to take greater control of their careers and financial destinies.

The gig economy's evolution doesn't stop at freelancing; it extends into the realm of investing. Gig workers, armed with the flexibility and financial independence gained from their side gigs, can strategically channel their earnings into investments that yield long-term returns. This shift marks a departure from merely working for money to letting money work for the gig worker.

Investing in the gig economy involves not only traditional financial investments but also leveraging skills, networks, and platforms. Gig workers can invest in expanding their skill set, building a personal brand, and strategically choosing lucrative gigs. This approach transforms gig work from a means of earning income into a holistic investment in one's professional and financial future.

In conclusion, the gig economy represents more than just a shift in how we work—it's a transformative force that opens doors to new possibilities. Embracing the flexibility of side gigs and recognizing the evolution from freelancing to investing empowers individuals to navigate this dynamic landscape with purpose and strategic intent. The gig economy is not just a job market; it's an ecosystem where the savvy gig worker can sow the seeds of financial growth and professional fulfillment.

CHAPTER 2: NAVIGATING THE GIG LANDSCAPE

In the vast and dynamic landscape of the gig economy, success lies not just in finding gigs but in navigating the terrain with strategic intent. This chapter serves as a compass, guiding you through the process of identifying lucrative side gig opportunities, assessing your skills and passions for gig success, and mastering the art of balancing multiple gigs for optimal returns.

Identifying Lucrative Side Gig Opportunities

The gig economy is a bustling marketplace with opportunities spanning a multitude of industries. Identifying the most lucrative side gig opportunities requires a combination of market awareness, self-reflection, and an understanding of your unique skill set.

Market Research: Stay informed about the trends and demands within the gig economy. What services are in high demand? Which industries are experiencing growth? Conducting thorough market research allows you to identify niches where your skills align with market needs, increasing the likelihood of finding lucrative opportunities.

Assessing Personal Skills: Take stock of your skills, both technical and soft. What are you exceptionally good at? What sets you apart from others in your field? Identifying your core competencies enables you to match your skills with opportunities that not only align with your expertise but also have high market demand.

Exploring Emerging Platforms: The gig economy constantly evolves, and new platforms emerge regularly. Explore a variety of gig platforms to discover where your skills are most valued. Whether it's freelancing websites, gig-specific apps, or industry-specific platforms, casting a wide net increases your chances of finding lucrative opportunities.

Networking: Leverage your professional and personal networks to uncover hidden opportunities. Networking not only provides insights into potential gigs but also allows you to learn from others who have successfully navigated the gig landscape. Attend industry events, engage in online forums, and connect with professionals to expand your gig horizons.

Analyzing Earning Potential: Assess the earning potential of different gig opportunities. Consider factors such as project complexity, time investment, and market rates. Prioritize gigs that offer a balance between financial reward and alignment with your skills and interests.

Assessing Your Skills and Passions for Gig Success

Success in the gig economy extends beyond financial gain; it's about finding fulfillment in the work you choose. Assessing your skills and passions not only enhances your overall job satisfaction but also positions you for sustained success in the gig landscape.

Skills Assessment: Conduct a comprehensive assessment of your skills, both technical and soft. Identify your strengths and areas for improvement. This self-awareness allows you to market your skills effectively and pursue gigs that align with your expertise.

Passion Alignment: Consider your passions and interests when selecting gig opportunities. Engaging in work that aligns with your passions not only enhances job satisfaction but also increases the likelihood of excelling in your chosen gigs. Passionate workers often go above and beyond, delivering exceptional results.

Identifying Transferable Skills: Explore how your existing skills can be transferred to different gig opportunities. The ability to apply your skills across various contexts not only expands your gig options but also positions you as a versatile and adaptable gig worker.

Continuous Learning: Invest in continuous learning to stay relevant in your chosen field. Attend workshops, enroll in online courses, and seek opportunities to enhance your skill set. Adapting to evolving industry trends ensures that your skills remain in demand, opening doors to a wider array of gig opportunities.

Feedback and Iteration: Seek feedback from clients and peers to refine and iterate on your skills. Constructive feedback provides valuable insights into areas for improvement and allows you to tailor your skills to meet the specific needs of the gig economy.

Balancing Multiple Gigs for Optimal Returns

While the gig economy offers the freedom to pursue multiple opportunities, striking the right balance is crucial for optimal returns. Juggling multiple gigs requires strategic planning, effective time management, and a keen awareness of your personal and professional limits.

Time Management: Develop a robust time management strategy to allocate sufficient time to each gig. Prioritize tasks, set realistic deadlines, and avoid overcommitting. Effective time management ensures that you can deliver quality work across multiple gigs without sacrificing your well-being.

Skill Synergy: Identify synergies between your gigs to maximize efficiency. If your gigs leverage similar skills or industry knowledge, you can capitalize on shared expertise, reducing the overall time and effort required for each gig.

Setting Boundaries: Establish clear boundaries to prevent burnout. Clearly communicate your availability to clients and set realistic expectations regarding deliverables and timelines. Setting boundaries ensures that you can maintain a sustainable workload without compromising the quality of your work.

Financial Planning: Implement a robust financial plan to manage income variability. Given the fluctuating nature of gig work, having a financial safety net and budgeting effectively are essential. Plan for periods of lower income and strategically allocate funds for both personal and professional needs.

Diversification: Diversify your gig portfolio to mitigate risks. Relying on a single source of income within the gig economy can be precarious. By diversifying the types of gigs you pursue, you create a more resilient income stream that can weather fluctuations in specific industries or markets.

In conclusion, navigating the gig landscape is an art that requires a blend of strategic thinking, self-awareness, and effective planning. Identifying lucrative side gig opportunities, assessing your skills and passions, and mastering the balance of multiple gigs set the stage for a successful and fulfilling journey in the gig economy. As you embark on this dynamic adventure, remember that each gig is an opportunity not just for financial gain but for personal and professional growth.

Chapter 3: The Investor's Mindset in the Gig Economy

In the vast expanse of the gig economy, adopting an investor's mindset is not just a strategic choice; it's a transformative shift that opens the door to wealth-building opportunities. This chapter explores the nuances of shifting from a worker to an investor mentality, evaluating risk and reward in gig investments, and leveraging gigs as building blocks for lasting financial prosperity.

Shifting from Worker to Investor Mentality

Traditionally, gig workers have approached their endeavors with a worker's mindset—a focus on completing tasks, earning income, and moving on to the next gig. Shifting to an investor mentality involves viewing each gig as an opportunity to not just earn money but to strategically invest in your long-term financial well-being.

Holistic Perspective: An investor's mindset requires a holistic perspective. Instead of viewing gigs in isolation, consider how each gig contributes to your overall financial portfolio. Recognize that every gig is a potential building block for wealth, and approach your work with an understanding of its broader impact on your financial goals.

Strategic Decision-Making: Investors make decisions with a long-term vision. Apply this principle to your gig choices. Evaluate the potential for ongoing work, skill development, and networking opportunities. Choose gigs that align with your overall financial strategy and contribute to the growth of your gig portfolio.

Risk Tolerance: Investors understand and manage risk. Assess the risk associated with each gig, considering factors such as market demand, payment stability, and the potential for future opportunities. A nuanced understanding of risk allows you to make informed decisions that align with your financial goals.

Diversification: Like a savvy investor diversifies their portfolio, diversify your gig endeavors. Engage in gigs that span different industries, skills, and platforms. Diversification not only reduces risk but also enhances your adaptability in a dynamic gig economy.

Reinvestment of Earnings: Investors reinvest their earnings to generate compounding returns. Apply this principle to your gig income. Instead of solely relying on gigs for immediate expenses, consider reinvesting a portion of your earnings into skill development, marketing, or tools that enhance your gig capabilities.

Evaluating Risk and Reward in Gig Investments

Every gig is an investment—of time, skills, and effort. Evaluating the risk and reward associated with each gig is a fundamental aspect of adopting an investor's mindset in the gig economy.

Market Analysis: Before accepting a gig, conduct a market analysis. Evaluate the demand for your skills, competition within the gig space, and the potential for growth. A thorough market analysis allows you to assess the viability of a gig and make informed decisions about its potential returns.

Payment Stability: Assess the stability of payments associated with a gig. Consider factors such as payment terms, frequency, and reliability of the gig platform or client. A stable payment structure reduces financial uncertainty and enhances the predictability of your income.

Long-Term Potential: Investors prioritize opportunities with long-term potential. Apply this principle to your gig choices by considering the scalability of the gig, the potential for recurring work, and the alignment of the gig with your evolving skills and interests. Pursue gigs that contribute to your long-term wealth-building goals.

Return on Investment (ROI): Evaluate the return on investment for each gig. Beyond monetary returns, consider the value of skills acquired, networking opportunities, and the potential for future referrals. A comprehensive assessment of ROI allows you to prioritize gigs that offer the most significant overall returns.

Adaptability: The gig economy is dynamic, with shifting trends and demands. Evaluate your adaptability to changes within your chosen gig space. A keen awareness of industry trends, emerging technologies, and evolving consumer needs positions you to make strategic decisions that align with the changing landscape of the gig economy.

Leveraging Gigs as Building Blocks for Wealth

Gigs, when approached with an investor's mindset, become powerful building blocks for wealth. The strategic combination of gigs, careful evaluation of risk and reward, and a focus on long-term goals lay the foundation for lasting financial prosperity.

Strategic Gig Portfolio: Build a strategic gig portfolio that aligns with your financial goals. Consider the synergy between different gigs, the potential for skill development, and the overall impact on your wealth-building strategy. Your gig portfolio should be a thoughtfully curated collection of opportunities that contribute to your financial success.

Continuous Learning: Invest in continuous learning as a means of enhancing your gig capabilities. Acquiring new skills not only makes you more valuable in the gig marketplace but also positions you for higher-paying opportunities. The ongoing investment in your skills becomes a key pillar in the construction of your wealth-building framework.

Networking and Relationships: Leverage gigs to build a robust professional network. Networking not only opens doors to new opportunities but also establishes your reputation within your chosen gig space. Strong professional relationships become invaluable assets in your wealth-building journey.

Reinvestment Strategies: Develop systematic reinvestment strategies for your gig earnings. Whether it's allocating funds for skill development, marketing, or tools that enhance your gig capabilities, strategic reinvestment contributes to the compounding growth of your wealth-building efforts.

Goal-Oriented Approach: Approach each gig with specific financial goals in mind. Whether it's saving for a major purchase, creating an emergency fund, or investing in long-term assets, align your gig endeavors with your financial aspirations. A goal-oriented approach transforms gigs from isolated tasks into intentional steps toward wealth creation.

CHAPTER 4: SMART INVESTMENTS FOR GIG INCOME

In the ever-evolving landscape of the gig economy, the savvy gig worker understands that earnings are not just for immediate expenses—they are a resource that can be strategically invested for long-term financial growth. This chapter delves into the realm of smart investments for gig income, guiding you through the exploration of investment options, the art of diversifying your portfolio with gig earnings, and the construction of a solid financial foundation through strategic investments.

Exploring Investment Options for Gig Workers

Gig workers, armed with a variable income stream, have a unique opportunity to explore a range of investment options tailored to their financial goals and risk tolerance. Here are key investment avenues to consider:

Stock Market Investments: Delve into the world of stocks, where you can invest in individual companies or diversified portfolios through exchange-traded funds (ETFs) or mutual funds. The stock market offers the potential for capital appreciation and dividends, providing gig workers with an opportunity to participate in the growth of global markets.

Real Estate: Consider real estate investments as a means of diversifying your portfolio. This can include purchasing rental properties, real estate crowdfunding, or investing in Real Estate Investment Trusts (REITs). Real estate investments have the potential for both ongoing rental income and property value appreciation.

Cryptocurrency: Explore the world of digital assets by considering investments in cryptocurrencies. While cryptocurrencies come with inherent risks, they also offer the potential for significant returns. Bitcoin, Ethereum, and other altcoins have gained popularity as alternative investment options.

Retirement Accounts: Prioritize contributions to retirement accounts, such as Individual Retirement Accounts (IRAs) or Simplified Employee Pension (SEP) IRAs. These tax-advantaged accounts provide a secure avenue for long-term savings, allowing gig workers to benefit from compounding returns and potential tax advantages.

Peer-to-Peer Lending: Participate in peer-to-peer lending platforms where you can lend money directly to individuals or small businesses. This alternative investment option can generate interest income and diversify your investment portfolio beyond traditional financial instruments.

Education and Skill Development: Consider investing in your own education and skill development. Enhancing your skill set not only increases your earning potential in the gig economy but also positions you for higher-paying opportunities and diversified gigs.

Diversifying Your Portfolio with Gig Earnings

Diversification is a cornerstone of sound financial planning, and gig workers can leverage their variable income to build a well-diversified investment portfolio. Diversifying your portfolio involves spreading your investments across different asset classes to reduce risk and optimize returns.

Asset Allocation: Allocate your gig earnings across a mix of asset classes, such as stocks, bonds, real estate, and cash equivalents. The right asset allocation depends on your financial goals, risk tolerance, and investment timeline.

Emergency Fund: Build and maintain an emergency fund as part of your diversified portfolio. This fund, typically held in liquid assets like savings accounts, provides a financial safety net for unexpected expenses or periods of lower gig income.

Gig-Specific Investments: Consider investments that align with your gig expertise. If you're a freelance graphic designer, for example, investing in design software, high-quality equipment, or online courses to enhance your skills could be a strategic use of gig earnings.

Recurring Investments: Implement a systematic approach to recurring investments. Set up automatic contributions to your investment accounts, allowing you to consistently invest a portion of your gig earnings without the need for manual intervention.

Risk Management: Mitigate risk through strategic diversification. Avoid concentrating too much of your gig income in one type of investment or sector. Diversification helps protect your portfolio from the volatility of specific assets and markets.

Regular Portfolio Review: Conduct regular reviews of your investment portfolio to ensure it aligns with your financial goals and risk tolerance. Adjust your asset allocation and investments as needed based on changes in the gig economy, market conditions, and your personal financial situation.

Building a Solid Financial Foundation through Strategic Investments

The ultimate goal of smart investments for gig workers is to build a solid financial foundation that withstands the dynamic nature of gig work and positions you for long-term success. Here's how to construct that foundation:

Define Financial Goals: Clearly define your financial goals, whether it's saving for a home, creating an emergency fund, or funding your retirement. Your goals serve as the guiding principles for your investment strategy.

Risk Assessment: Assess your risk tolerance and time horizon. Understanding how much risk you can comfortably bear and the length of time you plan to invest allows you to tailor your investments to your unique financial profile.

Emergency Fund: Prioritize the creation and maintenance of an emergency fund. This fund, typically covering three to six months of living expenses, provides a financial safety net during periods of income variability or unexpected expenses.

Automate Savings and Investments: Take advantage of automation to consistently save and invest a portion of your gig earnings. Set up automatic transfers to your savings and investment accounts to ensure that you prioritize financial goals even in the midst of a busy gig schedule.

Review and Adjust: Regularly review your investment portfolio and financial goals. Assess the performance of your investments, adjust your contributions based on changes in income, and realign your goals as your financial situation evolves.

Professional Guidance: Consider seeking guidance from financial professionals. A financial advisor can provide personalized advice based on your unique circumstances, helping you navigate the complexities of the gig economy and make informed investment decisions.

In conclusion, smart investments for gig income go beyond the traditional notions of earning and spending. By exploring diverse investment options, diversifying your portfolio, and strategically building a solid financial foundation, gig workers can transform their variable income into a powerful tool for long-term wealth creation. As you embark on this journey, remember that each strategic investment is a step closer to financial security and the fulfillment of your financial aspirations in the gig economy.

Chapter 5: Tax Strategies for Gig Investors

In the intricate dance of the gig economy, understanding and optimizing your tax strategy is akin to mastering the steps to a complex choreography. This chapter unravels the nuances of tax obligations in the gig economy, unveils the art of maximizing deductions for gig-related expenses, and advocates for the importance of consulting with financial professionals for tax optimization.

Navigating Tax Obligations in the Gig Economy

The gig economy's flexibility and autonomy come hand in hand with increased responsibility when it comes to taxes. Navigating tax obligations is a vital aspect of ensuring that gig investors can maximize their earnings while staying compliant with tax laws.

Familiarize Yourself with Tax Requirements: Gig workers often fall into the category of self-employed individuals. This means understanding and fulfilling self-employment tax obligations, which include Social Security and Medicare taxes. Familiarize yourself with the specific tax laws and deadlines relevant to your gig work.

Keep Meticulous Records: Maintaining accurate and detailed records is a fundamental part of navigating tax obligations in the gig economy. Keep track of your income, expenses, and any relevant documentation, such as 1099 forms received from clients or gig platforms. This meticulous record-keeping becomes invaluable during tax filing season.

Estimated Quarterly Payments: Unlike traditional employees who have taxes withheld from their paychecks, gig workers are typically responsible for making estimated quarterly tax payments. This proactive approach helps prevent a substantial tax burden at the end of the year and allows gig investors to manage their cash flow more effectively.

Stay Informed about Tax Deductions: Stay abreast of tax deductions available to gig workers. From home office expenses to business-related travel, understanding these deductions can significantly reduce taxable income. The more you know about eligible deductions, the more you can optimize your tax strategy.

Maximizing Deductions for Gig-Related Expenses

One of the key advantages for gig investors lies in the ability to maximize deductions for a plethora of expenses directly related to their gig work. Here's how you can make the most of these deductions:

Home Office Deduction: If you use a portion of your home exclusively for your gig work, you may be eligible for the home office deduction. This can include a percentage of your rent or mortgage, utilities, and other home-related expenses.

Business Supplies and Equipment: Deduct the cost of supplies and equipment necessary for your gig work. Whether it's a new computer, specialized tools, or materials required for your services, these expenses can be deducted to reduce your taxable income.

Professional Fees and Memberships: If you pay for professional memberships, subscriptions, or licenses relevant to your gig work, these costs are often deductible. Keep track of payments to industry organizations, online platforms, or any other professional association that enhances your gig endeavors.

Travel Expenses: If your gig involves travel, either locally or internationally, you may be able to deduct related expenses. This includes transportation, accommodation, meals, and other business-related travel costs. Be sure to keep thorough records of your travel activities and expenses.

Health Insurance Premiums: Gig workers who are not eligible for employer-sponsored health insurance can often deduct health insurance premiums. This deduction helps alleviate the financial burden of obtaining health coverage independently.

Consulting with Financial Professionals for Tax Optimization

While navigating tax obligations and maximizing deductions are crucial steps for gig investors, seeking the guidance of financial professionals can elevate your tax optimization strategy to new heights.

Engage a Certified Tax Professional: Collaborate with a certified tax professional who specializes in the complexities of gig and self-employment taxes. Their expertise can help you navigate the intricacies of tax laws, identify additional deductions, and ensure compliance with the latest regulations.

Strategic Tax Planning: Financial professionals can assist in developing a strategic tax planning approach tailored to your specific gig work. This may involve adjusting your estimated quarterly payments, exploring tax credits, or implementing advanced strategies to optimize your overall tax liability.

Year-Round Advice: Rather than treating tax season as an annual event, engage with financial professionals throughout the year. This ongoing collaboration allows for proactive tax planning, ensuring that your gig income is strategically managed from a tax perspective.

Audit Support: In the event of an audit or tax-related inquiry, having a financial professional on your side provides valuable support. They can guide you through the process, respond to inquiries, and ensure that you are well-equipped to address any tax-related challenges.

Incorporate Tax Efficiency into Financial Planning: Financial professionals can help you integrate tax efficiency into your broader financial planning. This holistic approach considers not only your immediate tax obligations but also long-term strategies to optimize your financial well-being.

In conclusion, mastering tax strategies for gig investors requires a combination of knowledge, diligence, and professional support. Navigating tax obligations, maximizing deductions, and consulting with financial professionals create a threefold strategy that empowers gig workers to optimize their tax position. As you waltz through the intricate steps of the gig economy, let your tax strategy be the well-practiced routine that ensures you keep more of your hard-earned income while staying in harmony with tax laws.

Chapter 6: Managing Finances for Gig Success

In the dynamic and ever-evolving realm of gig work, managing finances is not just a task; it's a strategic imperative for success. This chapter unfolds the essential components of managing finances for gig success, encompassing budgeting strategies tailored to the gig lifestyle, the importance of setting financial goals and milestones, and the establishment of emergency funds for financial security.

Budgeting Strategies for Gig Workers

Budgeting is the cornerstone of financial management, and for gig workers, it takes on a unique flavor. Here are effective budgeting strategies crafted to align with the dynamic nature of gig work:

Variable Income Planning: Embrace the variability of gig income by adopting a variable income budgeting approach. Instead of relying on a fixed monthly income, plan your budget based on a range of possible income scenarios. This proactive strategy helps mitigate financial stress during months of lower gig earnings.

Prioritize Essential Expenses: Identify and prioritize essential expenses, ensuring that your basic needs are met even in leaner months. Essentials include rent or mortgage, utilities, groceries, and healthcare. Allocating a specific portion of your income to these priorities provides a financial safety net.

Create a Flexible Spending Plan: Build flexibility into your spending plan to accommodate fluctuations in gig income. Allocate a portion of your budget to discretionary expenses, allowing you to adjust spending based on the variability of your monthly earnings.

Emergency Fund Contributions: Include contributions to your emergency fund as a non-negotiable part of your budget. Establishing and consistently funding an emergency fund provides a financial cushion for unexpected expenses or periods of lower gig income.

Track and Review Expenses: Regularly track and review your expenses to identify areas for optimization. Utilize budgeting apps or spreadsheets to categorize and analyze your spending habits. This ongoing assessment allows you to make informed decisions about your financial priorities.

Setting Financial Goals and Milestones

Setting clear financial goals and milestones is a compass that guides gig workers toward long-term success. Here's how to craft and pursue meaningful financial objectives:

Define Short-Term and Long-Term Goals: Distinguish between short-term and long-term financial goals. Short-term goals may include creating an emergency fund, paying off high-interest debt, or investing in essential tools for your gig work. Long-term goals could involve saving for a home, funding education, or building a retirement nest egg.

Prioritize Goals Based on Values: Align your financial goals with your values and priorities. This alignment ensures that your pursuit of financial objectives is not just about numbers but about creating a lifestyle that resonates with your aspirations and beliefs.

Establish Achievable Milestones: Break down larger financial goals into achievable milestones. These milestones serve as progress markers, providing a sense of accomplishment and motivation. Whether it's saving a specific amount, paying off a credit card, or reaching a certain income level, milestones make your financial journey tangible.

Incorporate Professional Development Goals: Recognize the value of investing in your skills and professional development as part of your financial goals. Allocate funds for courses, workshops, or certifications that enhance your gig capabilities and open doors to higher-paying opportunities.

Regularly Assess and Adjust Goals: Life in the gig economy is dynamic, and so too should be your financial goals. Regularly assess your goals, considering changes in income, industry trends, and personal priorities. Adjust your financial objectives to reflect your evolving circumstances and aspirations.

Establishing Emergency Funds for Financial Security

In the gig economy, where income can be variable and unpredictable, the establishment of emergency funds is not just a financial precaution; it's a pillar of stability. Here's how to build and maintain emergency funds for financial security:

Calculate Living Expenses: Determine the amount needed to cover essential living expenses for a specified period, typically three to six months. This includes rent or mortgage, utilities, groceries, healthcare, and other critical expenses.

Automate Contributions: Set up automated contributions to your emergency fund. Treat these contributions as non-negotiable expenses, just like any other essential bills. Automating the process ensures consistent and disciplined funding of your emergency fund.

Utilize Windfalls: Channel unexpected windfalls, such as tax refunds, gig bonuses, or unexpected income spikes, directly into your emergency fund. This strategic use of windfalls accelerates the growth of your fund without impacting your regular budget.

Replenish After Withdrawals: If you need to tap into your emergency fund for unforeseen expenses, make it a priority to replenish the withdrawn amount. This ensures that your emergency fund remains a robust financial safety net for future uncertainties.

Regularly Review and Adjust: Regularly review the adequacy of your emergency fund. Consider factors such as changes in living expenses, income fluctuations, or life events that may impact your financial needs. Adjust the target amount for your emergency fund based on these assessments.

In conclusion, managing finances for gig success is a multifaceted endeavor that requires adaptability, foresight, and disciplined financial habits. By implementing budgeting strategies that embrace the variability of gig income, setting meaningful financial goals and milestones, and establishing robust emergency funds, gig workers can navigate the dynamic landscape of the gig economy with confidence. As you embark on your financial journey in the gig world, let these strategies be your compass, guiding you toward financial stability, growth, and success.

CHAPTER 7: RETIREMENT PLANNING FOR GIG WORKERS

In the gig economy, where flexibility and autonomy reign supreme, the notion of retirement planning takes on a unique hue. This chapter unravels the intricacies of retirement planning for gig workers, guiding them through the creation of a tailored retirement plan, exploring self-employed retirement options, and finding the delicate balance between present enjoyment and future security.

Creating a Retirement Plan in the Gig Economy

Retirement planning is often perceived as a traditional nine-to-five endeavor, but for gig workers, it requires a bespoke approach that mirrors the fluidity of their work. Here's how to craft a retirement plan tailored to the gig lifestyle:

Understand Your Income Patterns: Given the variable nature of gig income, understanding your income patterns is the first step in creating a retirement plan. Assess your average monthly income and identify strategies to consistently set aside a portion for retirement savings.

Establish a Target Retirement Age: Define your target retirement age, keeping in mind the flexibility inherent in gig work. Whether you plan to retire early or work well into your golden years, having a clear target provides a timeline for your retirement savings goals.

Calculate Retirement Expenses: Estimate your retirement expenses by considering factors such as healthcare, housing, daily living costs, and any specific retirement goals you may have. Understanding your future financial needs allows you to set realistic savings targets.

Utilize Retirement Calculators: Leverage online retirement calculators to estimate how much you need to save for retirement. These tools consider factors such as expected rate of return, inflation, and life expectancy, providing insights into the level of savings required to maintain your desired lifestyle in retirement.

Diversify Retirement Investments: Embrace a diversified investment strategy for your retirement savings. Explore a mix of investment vehicles, including stocks, bonds, and other retirement-specific options, to optimize returns and manage risk.

Exploring Self-Employed Retirement Options

For gig workers, traditional employer-sponsored retirement plans are often replaced by self-employed retirement options. Understanding these alternatives is crucial for building a robust retirement strategy:

Solo 401(k): The Solo 401(k) is a powerful retirement option for self-employed individuals. It allows you to contribute as both the employer and the employee, potentially enabling higher contribution limits compared to other plans. The Solo 401(k) offers flexibility and a range of investment choices.

SEP IRA (Simplified Employee Pension Individual Retirement Account): The SEP IRA is a straightforward and tax-efficient retirement option for gig workers. It allows for tax-deductible contributions and is easy to set up. Contributions to a SEP IRA are made by the employer, making it suitable for solo entrepreneurs or small business owners.

SIMPLE IRA (Savings Incentive Match Plan for Employees): The SIMPLE IRA is designed for businesses with fewer than 100 employees, making it suitable for certain gig workers. It offers employer and employee contributions, providing a simplified yet effective retirement savings vehicle.

IRA (Individual Retirement Account): Traditional and Roth IRAs are popular choices for self-employed individuals. While not exclusive to gig workers, IRAs offer flexibility and a range of investment options. Traditional IRAs provide tax-deferred growth, while Roth IRAs offer tax-free withdrawals in retirement.

HSA (Health Savings Account): While primarily designed for healthcare expenses, the HSA can also serve as a retirement savings tool. Contributions are tax-deductible, and qualified withdrawals for medical expenses are tax-free. After age 65, non-medical withdrawals are subject to income tax without penalties.

Balancing Present Enjoyment with Future Security

One of the unique challenges for gig workers is striking the delicate balance between enjoying the present and securing their financial future. Here's how to navigate this balancing act:

Prioritize Retirement Contributions: While embracing the freedom of gig work, prioritize contributions to your retirement plan. Establish a habit of setting aside a portion of your income for retirement before indulging in discretionary spending. Consistent contributions ensure that your future remains a financial priority.

Set Realistic Spending Boundaries: Enjoying the present doesn't mean overspending. Set realistic spending boundaries that align with your financial goals. Budget for discretionary expenses while ensuring that retirement contributions and other savings remain intact.

Automate Savings: Automate your retirement contributions to make saving a seamless part of your financial routine. Automation reduces the temptation to spend money earmarked for retirement and ensures a disciplined approach to building your retirement nest egg.

Incorporate Flexible Financial Goals: Recognize that life in the gig economy is dynamic, and financial goals should be adaptable. Incorporate flexible financial goals that allow for present enjoyment without compromising your long-term security. This might include travel, skill development, or pursuing passion projects.

Regularly Assess and Adjust: Periodically assess your financial situation and retirement goals. Adjust your contributions and financial priorities based on changes in income, lifestyle, or personal aspirations. A dynamic approach ensures that your financial strategy evolves with the fluidity of gig work.

In conclusion, retirement planning for gig workers is a nuanced dance between present enjoyment and future security. Crafting a tailored retirement plan, exploring self-employed retirement options, and striking a delicate balance in spending and saving are essential steps in this journey. As you navigate the gig economy, let your retirement strategy be a harmonious blend of financial responsibility and the freedom to enjoy the fruits of your labor today and in the years to come.

Chapter 8: Building a Brand as a Gig Investor

In the bustling landscape of the gig economy, where individuality is celebrated and entrepreneurship is the heartbeat, building a brand isn't reserved for big corporations—it's a potent tool for gig investors. This chapter unravels the art of establishing your personal brand in the gig economy, delves into strategies for marketing your skills to maximize gig opportunities, and explores the dynamic realm of leveraging social media for gig visibility and networking.

Establishing Your Personal Brand in the Gig Economy

Your personal brand is the unique tapestry that sets you apart in the gig economy. It's not just about what you do; it's about how you do it and the story you tell. Here's how to craft and establish your personal brand:

Define Your Unique Value Proposition: What sets you apart from the myriad of gig workers in your field? Identify your unique value proposition—the combination of skills, experiences, and qualities that make you stand out. This is the foundation of your personal brand.

Craft a Compelling Narrative: Your personal brand is a story, and every story needs a compelling narrative. Define the story you want to tell about your journey, expertise, and the value you bring to clients. Make it authentic, relatable, and aligned with your goals.

Clarify Your Target Audience: Know your audience—the clients and collaborators you want to attract. Understanding their needs, preferences, and pain points allows you to tailor your brand messaging to resonate with the right people.

Create a Consistent Visual Identity: Visuals matter in the gig economy. Develop a consistent visual identity, including a professional logo, color palette, and imagery that reflects your brand. Consistency across platforms builds brand recognition.

Showcase Testimonials and Success Stories: Let the success stories of your gigs speak for themselves. Showcase testimonials from satisfied clients, share case studies of successful projects, and highlight the impact of your work. Authentic endorsements build trust in your brand.

Marketing Your Skills for Maximum Gig Opportunities

In the gig economy, marketing is not just reserved for products—it's about marketing your skills, expertise, and the value you bring to the table. Here's how to market yourself effectively for maximum gig opportunities:

Optimize Your Online Presence: Your online presence is your virtual storefront. Ensure that your professional profiles on platforms like LinkedIn, Upwork, or other gig-focused sites are polished, up-to-date, and highlight your skills and experience. Use keywords relevant to your niche for better discoverability.

Build a Portfolio: A portfolio is your visual resume in the gig economy. Create a comprehensive portfolio showcasing your best work, projects, and achievements. Include before-and-after examples, case studies, and any relevant metrics that demonstrate the impact of your contributions.

Niche Down: While the gig economy celebrates versatility, niching down can enhance your marketability. Identify a specific niche or expertise within your broader field. This not only makes you more attractive to clients looking for specialized skills but also reduces competition in your specific area.

Invest in Skill Development: Continuous skill development is a form of self-marketing. Stay abreast of industry trends, acquire new skills, and invest in certifications that enhance your expertise. This proactive approach positions you as a forward-thinking gig worker.

Network Strategically: Networking is a powerful marketing tool in the gig economy. Attend industry events, join online communities, and actively engage with peers and potential clients. Networking opens doors to collaborations, referrals, and valuable insights into gig opportunities.

Leveraging Social Media for Gig Visibility and Networking

In the digital age, social media is a dynamic arena for gig visibility and networking. Here's how to harness the power of social media to elevate your personal brand and expand your gig network:

Choose the Right Platforms: Not all social media platforms are created equal. Choose platforms that align with your target audience and industry. LinkedIn is a go-to for professional networking, while platforms like Instagram or Twitter may be more suitable for creative fields.

Optimize Your Profiles: Treat your social media profiles as extensions of your personal brand. Optimize your bio, use professional profile pictures, and ensure consistency in your branding across platforms. A cohesive online presence enhances your credibility.

Share Valuable Content: Position yourself as an industry expert by sharing valuable content related to your niche. Create and curate content that showcases your knowledge, solves problems, or sparks discussions. Consistent sharing establishes you as a thought leader.

Engage Authentically: Social media is not a one-way street. Engage authentically with your audience by responding to comments, participating in discussions, and sharing insights. Authentic engagement builds a community around your brand.

Showcase Behind-the-Scenes: Humanize your brand by offering glimpses behind the scenes. Share your work process, milestones, and even challenges. Authenticity fosters connections, and connections can translate into gig opportunities.

Participate in Relevant Hashtags and Challenges: Leverage trending hashtags and challenges in your industry. Participating in relevant conversations and challenges increases the visibility of your posts and exposes your brand to a broader audience.

In conclusion, building a brand as a gig investor is a multifaceted endeavor that combines personal branding, skill marketing, and social media savvy. By establishing a compelling personal brand, marketing your skills strategically, and leveraging social media for visibility and networking, you position yourself not just as a gig worker but as a brand that stands out in the bustling landscape of the gig economy. As you embark on this journey of self-promotion, remember that your personal brand is the compass that guides clients and collaborators to choose you over the myriad options available in the gig marketplace.

CHAPTER 9: SCALING UP: FROM SIDE GIG TO MAIN INCOME

In the dynamic landscape of the gig economy, the transition from a side gig to a main income is a transformative journey that requires strategic planning, a sustainable business model, and a keen understanding of balancing risk and reward. This chapter explores the strategies for transitioning gigs into full-time ventures, delves into the intricacies of building a sustainable gig business model, and provides insights into the delicate art of balancing risk and reward in the expansion of your gig endeavors.

Strategies for Transitioning Gigs into Full-Time Ventures

Making the leap from side gigs to a main income stream is a significant step that demands careful consideration and intentional strategies. Here's how to navigate this transition effectively:

Assess Market Demand: Before committing to a full-time gig venture, assess the demand for your services or products. Is there consistent and growing demand? Understanding the market dynamics ensures that your transition is supported by a viable and sustainable market.

Financial Preparedness: Assess your financial readiness for the transition. Calculate your current and projected income from the gig, factoring in potential fluctuations. Ensure that you have a financial safety net to cover living expenses during the initial stages of full-time gigging.

Diversify Revenue Streams: Consider diversifying your revenue streams within the gig. Explore complementary services, products, or collaborations that align with your core gig but offer additional income opportunities. Diversification enhances financial stability.

Build a Client Base: A robust client base is the bedrock of a successful full-time gig venture. Cultivate strong relationships with existing clients and actively seek new ones. A stable and expanding client base provides a consistent flow of work and income.

Optimize Time Management: Transitioning to full-time gigging often requires optimizing your time management skills. Efficiently allocate your time to different aspects of your gig business, including client work, marketing, and administrative tasks. Time optimization enhances productivity and income generation.

Building a Sustainable Gig Business Model

A sustainable business model is the backbone of a full-time gig venture. Here's how to build a model that ensures longevity and growth:

Define Your Value Proposition: Clearly articulate the value you bring to clients. Your value proposition should address their needs, solve their problems, or enhance their experiences. A compelling value proposition sets the foundation for sustainable client relationships.

Set Competitive Pricing: Price your services or products competitively. Consider factors such as market rates, your expertise, and the perceived value you provide. Competitive pricing not only attracts clients but also ensures that your gig remains financially viable.

Invest in Professional Development: Stay ahead of the curve by continually investing in your professional development. Enhance your skills, stay informed about industry trends, and adapt to evolving market demands. A proactive approach to professional development positions your gig for sustained success.

Create Scalable Processes: Design your gig operations with scalability in mind. Implement processes that can handle increased workloads without sacrificing quality. Scalable processes enable you to grow your gig business efficiently.

Establish Clear Financial Goals: Set clear financial goals for your gig business. Define revenue targets, expense thresholds, and profitability benchmarks. Regularly assess your financial performance against these goals and adjust your business strategies accordingly.

Balancing Risk and Reward in Gig Expansion

Expansion comes with inherent risks, but strategic balancing of risk and reward can pave the way for sustainable growth. Here's how to navigate this delicate equilibrium:

Conduct Risk Assessments: Identify potential risks associated with gig expansion. This may include financial risks, market risks, or operational risks. Conduct thorough risk assessments to understand potential challenges and develop mitigation strategies.

Pilot New Offerings: Before full-scale expansion, pilot new offerings or ventures on a smaller scale. This allows you to test the market response, refine your offerings, and minimize the financial risks associated with untested ventures.

Diversify Client Portfolio: Relying on a small number of clients poses a risk to the stability of your gig business. Diversify your client portfolio to reduce the impact of client-specific challenges. A diverse client base enhances resilience and mitigates the risk of revenue fluctuations.

Monitor Industry Trends: Stay vigilant to industry trends and market shifts. Anticipate changes that could impact your gig business and adjust your strategies accordingly. Being proactive in adapting to industry trends helps you stay ahead of potential risks.

Maintain Financial Resilience: Building financial resilience is crucial when expanding your gig business. Maintain a healthy financial cushion to weather unforeseen challenges. Financial resilience provides the flexibility to navigate uncertainties without compromising the core of your gig venture.

In conclusion, scaling up from a side gig to a main income requires a strategic blend of transitioning strategies, sustainable business models, and a nuanced understanding of risk and reward. By carefully assessing market demand, building a sustainable gig business model, and balancing risks during expansion, you position your gig for not just growth but long-term success. As you embark on this transformative journey, let each strategic move be a calculated step toward realizing the full potential of your gig as a main income source.

CHAPTER 10: NAVIGATING CHALLENGES IN THE GIG ECONOMY

The gig economy, with its promises of flexibility and autonomy, also presents a unique set of challenges that gig workers must navigate. From job insecurity and income fluctuations to the ever-present specter of burnout, and the impact of economic downturns and industry shifts, this chapter addresses the multifaceted challenges that gig workers encounter and offers insights on overcoming them.

Addressing Job Insecurity and Income Fluctuations

One of the defining features of the gig economy is the inherent job insecurity and income fluctuations. Gig workers often grapple with the unpredictability of work availability and the instability of income streams. Here's how to address these challenges:

Diversify Your Gig Portfolio: Instead of relying on a single gig, diversify your portfolio. Engage in multiple gigs or offer various services within your expertise. This approach helps mitigate the impact of job insecurity in one area by balancing it with stability in others.

Create an Emergency Fund: Job insecurity is more manageable when you have a financial safety net. Establish and consistently contribute to an emergency fund that covers living expenses for a designated period. This fund acts as a buffer during lean periods.

Network and Build Relationships: Cultivate a strong professional network. Building relationships within your industry can lead to a steady flow of opportunities. Networking provides a support system and opens doors to new gigs, reducing the impact of job insecurity.

Stay Agile and Adaptable: Embrace the agile mindset. The ability to adapt to changing circumstances is a valuable asset in the gig economy. Be open to learning new skills, exploring emerging trends, and pivoting when necessary.

Overcoming Burnout in a Gig-Driven World

The freedom and flexibility of the gig economy can sometimes blur the boundaries between work and personal life, leading to burnout. Overcoming burnout requires intentional strategies to maintain a healthy work-life balance:

Establish Clear Boundaries: Set clear boundaries between work and personal time. Designate specific working hours and stick to them. Communicate these boundaries to clients and collaborators, ensuring that they respect your off-hours.

Prioritize Self-Care: Prioritize self-care to prevent burnout. Incorporate regular breaks, exercise, and moments of relaxation into your routine. Taking care of your physical and mental well-being is essential for sustained productivity and creativity.

Delegate or Outsource Tasks: Recognize when it's time to delegate or outsource tasks. Trying to do everything yourself can lead to burnout. Delegate non-core tasks to free up your time for high-impact activities.

Schedule Time Off: Just as you would in a traditional job, schedule regular time off. Whether it's a day, a weekend, or a longer vacation, taking breaks is crucial for rejuvenation. Use this time to recharge and come back to your gigs with renewed energy.

Coping with Economic Downturns and Industry Shifts

The gig economy is not immune to economic downturns and industry shifts. Coping with these challenges requires a combination of strategic planning and adaptability:

Create a Financial Contingency Plan: Anticipate economic downturns by creating a financial contingency plan. Identify areas where you can cut expenses if needed and develop strategies to navigate lean periods. A well-thought-out plan provides a roadmap for financial resilience.

Stay Informed About Industry Trends: Keep a pulse on industry trends and market shifts. Being informed allows you to anticipate changes in demand for your services or products. Stay proactive in adapting your gig strategies to align with evolving industry dynamics.

Diversify Across Industries: If your gig allows for it, consider diversifying across industries. Having a presence in multiple sectors can help buffer the impact of downturns in one industry by leveraging stability in others.

Invest in Continuous Learning: Stay ahead of industry shifts by investing in continuous learning. Acquiring new skills positions you as a valuable asset in changing markets. Attend workshops, take online courses, and stay informed about emerging trends.

Network Strategically: Strategic networking is especially crucial during economic downturns. Build relationships with professionals across industries, attend industry events, and stay connected with your network. Networking can uncover new opportunities and provide valuable insights into industry shifts.

CHAPTER 11: SOCIAL IMPACT INVESTING IN THE GIG ECONOMY

In the expansive realm of the gig economy, where individual pursuits often take center stage, there's a growing movement toward social impact investing. This chapter delves into the unique intersection of gig opportunities and social impact, guiding gig workers on how to explore ventures that align with a greater purpose. We'll navigate the delicate balance between profit and purpose in gig ventures and explore the transformative potential of creating positive change through gig investments.

Exploring Gig Opportunities with Social Impact

Gig opportunities with social impact go beyond the conventional realms of profit generation. They involve leveraging skills and passions to contribute positively to society. Here's how gig workers can explore opportunities that make a meaningful difference:

Identify Social Causes: Start by identifying social causes or issues that resonate with you. Whether it's environmental sustainability, social justice, or community development, aligning your gig with a cause you're passionate about adds a deeper layer of purpose to your work.

Research Socially Conscious Platforms: Explore gig platforms that prioritize social impact. These platforms connect gig workers with projects and organizations dedicated to making a difference. From freelance writing for nonprofits to designing for social enterprises, these opportunities blend work with a higher purpose.

Collaborate with Impact-Driven Clients: Seek out clients who prioritize social impact. Many businesses, both large and small, are incorporating social responsibility into their operations. Collaborating with impact-driven clients allows gig workers to contribute to positive change through their expertise.

Offer Skill-Based Volunteering: Consider offering your skills pro bono to causes you believe in. Skill-based volunteering allows you to use your professional expertise for social good. This could involve providing marketing services to a local community initiative or offering financial advice to a nonprofit organization.

Balancing Profit and Purpose in Gig Ventures

Balancing profit and purpose is a delicate art, especially in the gig economy where financial sustainability often takes precedence. Here's how gig workers can navigate this balance:

Define Your Values: Clearly define your values and priorities. Understand what matters most to you in terms of both profit and purpose. This clarity serves as a compass, guiding you toward gig opportunities that align with your overarching goals.

Set Impact Goals: Establish impact goals alongside financial goals. Determine the level of social impact you want to achieve through your gig ventures. This could be measured in terms of environmental sustainability, community engagement, or contributions to specific social causes.

Research Ethical Business Practices: When considering gigs, research the ethical practices of potential clients or platforms. Opt for opportunities that align with your values and demonstrate a commitment to ethical and socially responsible business practices.

Negotiate Fair Compensation: Recognize the value of your skills and expertise. While engaging in social impact work, don't compromise on fair compensation. By negotiating fair payment, you contribute to the sustainability of your gig and ensure that your efforts are recognized and valued.

Creating Positive Change Through Gig Investments

Gig investments have the potential to extend beyond personal gain, creating a ripple effect of positive change. Here's how gig workers can actively contribute to creating positive change through their investments:

Measure Impact Metrics: Define specific metrics to measure the impact of your gig investments.

Whether it's the number of lives touched, environmental benefits, or community development milestones, having quantifiable metrics allows you to track and communicate the positive change generated.

Share Impact Stories: Showcase the impact of your gig investments through storytelling. Share success stories, testimonials, and tangible outcomes that highlight the positive change your work has contributed to. Storytelling not only inspires others but also amplifies the reach of your impact.

Collaborate with Like-Minded Giggers: Connect with other gig workers who share a commitment to social impact. Collaborate on projects or initiatives that collectively contribute to positive change. The synergy of like-minded giggers can amplify the impact of individual efforts.

Invest in Sustainable Practices: Integrate sustainable practices into your gig work. From reducing environmental footprints to supporting fair labor practices, incorporating sustainability into your gig ventures contributes to positive change both locally and globally.

Educate and Advocate: Use your platform as a gig worker to educate others about the importance of social impact. Advocate for ethical practices in the gig economy and encourage clients and platforms to prioritize socially responsible initiatives.

In conclusion, social impact investing in the gig economy represents a powerful avenue for gig workers to align their skills and passions with positive change. By exploring gig opportunities with social impact, balancing profit and purpose in gig ventures, and actively creating positive change through gig investments, gig workers can contribute to a more sustainable and socially responsible future. As you embark on this journey, let the impact of your gig work extend beyond financial gains, leaving a lasting legacy of positive change in the communities and causes you touch.

CHAPTER 12: MINDFUL SUCCESS IN THE GIG ECONOMY

In the bustling world of the gig economy, where hustle culture and constant connectivity prevail, achieving success isn't merely about financial gains—it's about cultivating a mindful approach that prioritizes well-being and sustainability. This chapter explores the art of mindful success in the gig economy, guiding gig workers on how to invest with mindfulness, balance financial success with personal well-being, and nurture a lifestyle that sustains both professional and personal fulfillment.

Cultivating a Mindful Approach to Gig Investing

Gig investing goes beyond the traditional understanding of financial returns; it encompasses the holistic impact of your work on your well-being and the world around you. Here's how to cultivate a mindful approach to gig investing:

Align Investments with Values: Before taking on a gig, reflect on whether it aligns with your values and goals. Consider the social, environmental, and personal implications of the work. Choosing gigs that resonate with your values enhances the overall satisfaction derived from your professional endeavors.

Set Intentional Goals: Define intentional goals for your gig investments. Instead of solely focusing on financial metrics, set goals that encompass personal growth, skill development, and positive contributions to the community or causes you care about.

Intentional goals add depth and purpose to your gig work.

Practice Presence in Work: Embrace mindfulness in the process of gig work. Practice being fully present in each task, immersing yourself in the work at hand. This not only enhances the quality of your output but also fosters a sense of fulfillment and connection with your craft.

Regularly Reflect on Impact: Periodically reflect on the impact of your gig investments. Assess not only the financial outcomes but also the broader effects on your well-being, relationships, and the community. Mindful reflection allows you to adjust your approach and continue evolving toward a more purposeful gig practice.

Balancing Financial Success with Personal Well-being

The pursuit of financial success in the gig economy often comes at the cost of personal well-being. Achieving a harmonious balance requires intentional strategies to safeguard your mental, emotional, and physical health:

Set Boundaries: Establish clear boundaries between work and personal life. Define specific working hours, adhere to breaks, and resist the urge to constantly check work-related notifications. Setting boundaries creates a healthy separation that preserves personal time and reduces burnout.

Prioritize Self-Care Rituals: Prioritize self-care as a non-negotiable aspect of your routine. Incorporate rituals that rejuvenate your mind and body, whether it's a morning meditation, regular exercise, or moments of creative expression. Consistent self-care enhances resilience and well-being.

Schedule Time for Personal Pursuits: Allocate dedicated time for personal pursuits outside of work. Whether it's a hobby, spending time with loved ones, or engaging in activities that bring you joy, scheduling time for personal pursuits reinforces the importance of a well-rounded life.

Regularly Assess Workload: Assess your workload regularly to prevent overwhelm. Understand your capacity and avoid taking on more gigs than you can manage without sacrificing your well-being. Quality work is sustainable only when balanced with a manageable workload.

Nurturing a Sustainable Gig Economy Lifestyle

Sustainability in the gig economy extends beyond individual gigs—it encompasses the lifestyle you cultivate. Here's how to nurture a sustainable gig economy lifestyle:

Diversify Income Streams: Avoid reliance on a single source of income. Diversify your gig portfolio to create a more stable and resilient income stream. This approach safeguards against fluctuations in specific gigs or industries.

Invest in Continuous Learning: Prioritize continuous learning to stay relevant and adaptable. Invest in acquiring new skills that align with emerging trends in your industry. A commitment to learning enhances your professional growth and longevity in the ever-evolving gig landscape.

Build a Support Network: Cultivate a support network within the gig community. Connect with fellow gig workers, share experiences, and offer mutual support. Building a community provides valuable insights, emotional support, and a sense of camaraderie in the gig journey.

Regularly Evaluate Lifestyle Choices: Periodically assess your lifestyle choices in relation to your gig work. Evaluate whether your current practices contribute to long-term well-being and sustainability. Adjust lifestyle choices that may hinder your ability to thrive both personally and professionally.

In conclusion, mindful success in the gig economy is a holistic pursuit that transcends financial gains. By cultivating a mindful approach to gig investing, balancing financial success with personal well-being, and nurturing a sustainable gig economy lifestyle, you embark on a journey that not only propels your professional endeavors but also fosters a life rich in purpose and fulfillment. As you navigate the gig landscape, let mindfulness be your guiding principle, ensuring that each gig contributes not only to your financial success but also to the sustainable and meaningful life you aspire to lead.

Milton Keynes UK
Ingram Content Group UK Ltd.
UKHW020237221123
432980UK00016B/1217